Death In The Holy Month

Death In The Holy Month

Sufia Khatoon

HAWAKAL PUBLISHERS

Published by **Hawakal Publishers**, 185, Kali Temple Road,
Nimta, Calcutta 700049, India.

Website: www.hawakal.com
Contact: info@hawakal.com

First edition (India): December, 2018

Printed and bound at *S. P. Communications,*
Kolkata

Cover art: Sufia Khatoon
Cover design: Bitan Chakraborty
Illustrations: Sufia Khatoon

ISBN-13: 978-93-87883-43-7

Price: INR 300/- [USD 10.00]

To *ammi*, Shabnam Begum, for empowering my words
To *nani*, Quamrun Nisa, for being my story-teller
To my siblings, *Nazia* and *Imran*, for being my pillars
To words for always being there for me
To the hard times for shaping me and to life for being
a source of inspiration

Contents

Nothing is dark,
only a flicker remains in places
where hope dies and lives every day
and everything else is constant in a moving world.

Critical Acclaim

Death in the Holy Month is Sufia Khatoon's debut collection of well-wrought poems that are a fine blend of striking visual imagery and sensitive word-play. The vivid images in the poems ranging from "gray-haired soul" to a "toothless child with a dream" express love, loss, longing, anguish and angst. Remarkably, the poems also subtly express a zest for life that transcends world-weariness and outrage. Sufia's poems will engross and enrich readers as they perceive that in the holy Month the "ladder of hope" is a beacon of assurance and inspiration.

Sanjukta Dasgupta

Sufia explores with lucidity the sensory nature of contemplation and memory. Very close to earth, she not just inhales soil, but listens to the galloping hoofs of rain for war and silence in the fragility of fruit and petal, prayer and wood-smoke.

Rochelle Potkar

In the days when raw spontaneity ruled over the world of good versification and even great poets had their overflow of emotions dammed in stanzas, from a forgotten locality where synecdoches lurk at every corner and metaphors grow wild, comes this quaint and paradoxically modern poet wet from the perennial fountains of death and grief and yet basking in the rays of hope. *Death in the Holy Month* grips your heart and the words ask you "What is life if not this?" These are the echoes of a poet's arrival.

Amit Shankar Saha

Personal agony merges with wounds of common people. Sufia converts her 'self' into the universal soul.

Kiriti Sengupta

Foreword

Sufia's world, that is Sufia Khatoon's collection of poems, *Death in the Holy Month*, addresses personal and spiritual quests. All the poems in the book, words singing into poems, spring from the enchantment of search between possibility and reality.

Nostalgia and memory jostle with each other making most of the poems sepia-tinted. Of course there are dashes and dots of cerulean and vermillion.

In this collection the poet experiments with language to express the fractured yet vibrant experiences of life, especially in her poems *Empty Room* and *Believe that My Skin Smells of Uprooted Longings*.

"If longing had a face, a similar fragrance,
the warmth of touch,
I wouldn't have been looking for it in empty rooms."

("Empty Room")

The infinite, the formless which makes the interior of life is ephemeral and hence sought after. More so, in a metropolis where everybody is running and interested in furnishing the exterior of life.

"Believe that the colour of my feet is turquoise blue,
bathing in salty tears of the never ending war of egos;
the sparkle in my eyes is the numbness of feelings
and my spirit is a blue rose forever loved by a unicorn,
grazing in your neighbourhood."

("Believe that My Skin Smells of Uprooted Longings")

As one progresses through the poems an uncanny
feeling overpowers the reader as if there is some
screaming going on inside the poet's head, an impossible
record that needs to be changed bringing in ochre light
that can play over and over on the physical spine of
reminiscence and catacombs of existence.

There is something touching about the poems-
something that eternally pleads for compassion, prayers
that are affirmations for laughs in the afternoon and
gaiety in the last leg of the summer giving away to
monsoon.

Sufia follows where her dreams lead, making the picture
into steps that lead to other representations, unfolding
like a Japanese fan and the metaphors create visible
images with a taste of life that is hard to forget.

Passionate and sardonic this poet has a taste for crisp
unpretentious lines of verse, often drawing together the
naïve and the sophisticated, so when one finishes reading
her poems there is a mixed sensation of exhilaration
and anti-climax.

Altogether an interesting read, but it must be read in a
lento mode.

Sharmila Ray
Kolkata

The Essence Of Life And Death

You can never truly understand pain. Why it emerges from the crevices of our mind and travels throughout the body? Why it finds the unattended wounds and makes you painfully aware of it? What it tries to tell you in the moments you aren't able to understand the cause of this never ending pain?

This book is my journey of understanding my own pain and the pain of others. When I write poems, I forget 'the self' and somehow my own existence takes a backstage. I am able to find the nerve and intensity of this pain and write on them. This gives hope to others and gives me warmth and comfort in return. It is remarkable how pain binds us all and teaches us to survive it. You just have to find your medium, your center of strength and go forward in life.

My soul has always been guided by the universal power; I call it Nature and the all merciful Allah. How do we get guided by it? It is only with faith in oneself and faith in the universal love. Even though at times, I am unable to understand the chaos of life and death, the violence of thoughts and insensitivity of people, the restlessness and emptiness within that keeps growing with time; I have realized that the purpose of life is living in its simplicity. We can't question the nature of things and the moment we do so, the storm rises. But a poet questions everything and poetry is more of a reflection of the universal truth and a reflection of within.

Where do I begin to recollect the whirlwind of the poetic essence that has changed my life and the lives I have witnessed?

Poetry is one such medium through which I have been able to awaken my quest of spirituality and understand the true essence of life and death.

Having experienced grief and death of so many close family members, growing used to the pain of losing good health and strength, understanding layers of this world and its workings, the sense of being rootless, finding myself and preserving my soul, that I got deeper in the quest of understanding death, God, life and everything travelling with time in this cycle. And in doing so, I understood that it was really important to understand pain and find a place to heal the wounds.

As if I was beginning to accept this chaos within and outside of me and healing it with each poem I experienced and wrote.

And like all languages, poetry became my prayer to God and the people to become one and heal themselves.

After collecting the memories, both good and sad and writing them down, I came to a conclusion that life is about hope and the only hope of living this life is living it truly. As God has stated that this life would be full of trails, so gather your strength, gather your hope and just live this life.

I hope after reading and experiencing this book of mine, you will be hopeful about taking this life as it comes, dealing with your pain, and healing through it all.

Love.

Sufia Khatoon
December 4, 2018
Kolkata

October Hibiscus

My back against the sun
I sit under the stairs and gaze
massaging the remains of words.

A pair of white doves
grazing in the cauliflower clouds
fill my heart with languish and longing.

It is the sweet smell of cookies and laughter in the air
and the kites gliding against the song
I knew as a child.

Mother is digging
adding seeds to soil and some care too.
October hibiscus didn't bloom in her garden
she worries, "They die untimely death."

Last night I felt the fear of death.
9-am-flowers still half-awake, eavesdrop
in my glass of poetry
in invited evening's chanting
I feel life breathing now.

My dried menstrual blood
flakes off my ankle
in the rays that touch everyone.

I pray and feel the assumptions seeping away
and my eyes touch the far distant minaret of the mosque.

Orange Skin

My skin is orange
slowly losing the pulp
decreasing, decaying.

The orange dress hangs
perspiring, stinking,
a reminder of my flesh.

Sides torn revealing
the orange insomnia,
I once was.

Under the orange sun
setting below my window
I sit to dry my soul
it was wet with longing.

The colour of solitude
painted well on my face
was content to reach its end.

Wrinkled marigold on the picture
smelled of a forgotten summer

when the fire of passion was alive
and the colour of love was orange.

Empty Rooms

If longing had a face, a similar fragrance,
the warmth of touch,
I wouldn't have been looking for it in empty rooms.

The rooms travel in between days and nights,
light and dark, frequenting in silence,
between my last memory of the Eid with my sister
and this Eid with her longing.

I found a picture of her and 'us,'
almost away and almost close,
hanging from the wall windows
in laughter and voices of wisdom.

The shared dresses and empty screams,
the picture of her innocent childhood in my eyes
tracing the memory on the cycle seat of my brother.

Now I imagine her strength seeping
through the windows when I have no one to talk to,
no one to fall back on.

"What's now the matter?" she enquires
and I cry with the longings of my dreams.
Analyzing the moments
I aspired to be beyond myself-
be beyond the human frailty and become her strength.

Her empty rooms none know
none can see through except those words close to her
I wish to be those words filling the rooms
with a day of 'us' again.

Ageless Ego

Ego, *maan, obhimaan, aanah*

I find the ageless ego growing its roots
beyond the soil of soul
and humility coils back in its shell.

When dandelions slept in my palms
and angst became a lion eating the yellow sun
I became that child without shame running around
naked,
looking again for my lost toys.

No clouds around, no hands to hold,
no voice echoing in the speechless storm.
Looking back at the time
when my fancies were my only friends.

The French window opens in a page
from my favourite story
and a sip of the sharp afternoon melts my emptiness.

This day was the day I was innocent

I had mercy and I had love,
but now all I have is anger seeping in
the story of violence.

The symphonies of words with a shrill cry
breaks the urn that claims to be human.

Humans were a thing of the past
now only objects live and breathe
often resurfacing as ageless ego.

Seasons Of Death And Mangoes

It's the summer of mangoes–1991,
I sit and savour a bowl of it.
My grandfather brings out his stick
in the courtyard
and chases me away from the delight,
he says, "Too much of it kills the soul."

Summer of 2018–
ripened mango oozing
out of my lips.
I look for my grandfather's stick again
to drive away the fear from my soul
the fear of the afterlife's uncanny aftertaste.

Cancer was what ate him away,
"What eats life?" I ask.

Sometimes I feel like throwing away everything
and become that child again.
The toothless child with a grin,
holding her fragmented face.

She had smelled of baby skin and
felt like the warm quilt in rain,
but the waterbed could never help her sleep
as she lay naked in her wakefulness.
Counting the days of the season of death
she smelled of nothingness then
and forgetful memories.

I search for her lost letters
and the soft fingers to hold now,
I ask, "What eats memories?"

In the blue of the fasting month
I prayed and cried
world had forgotten to love and be kind—
the month of 'memories of death' was upon me.

I had written a letter to God once,
asking for a miracle,
a baby brother—
his hands moved in the little box of thoughts
distinctively visible in the gloomy barricaded glass wall.

I stood waiting for his warm smile
on the other side
but the clots of anger choked what was left of prayers
and I never saw his innocent face.

I didn't hold him in my arms.
He passed away without tasting life,
I ask, "What eats innocence?"

If I could trade the world for silence,

I would purchase peace and lock myself inside it.
In the warmth of her embrace,
in his smile, in God's power
and float away into oblivion.

Believe that it never happened.
Nothing ever mattered or made sense
and the scared soul never cried.

Never felt weak or never felt death
"What eats hope?" I ask.

God Is Not For War

Magrib azaan settles on the dark walls.
Mother's prayer beads move through my thoughts
she prays with them, and says,
"God is not for war."

I collect feathers,
they have lesser concern
with the aftertaste of violence.

Can a day be beautiful?
No one has ever asked me that.
I don't let them, I show them instead.

If you walk your afternoons
you can find some have strained out
of your mind and
settled on the dusty old banyan tree.

It has felt the heart of dead cities and
it has lived a peaceful life.

Have I drifted away?

Or has the earth stopped moving for a night?
Some questions haunt me though
I feel it needs more consciousness.

My eyes resemble the icy well
such a waste of divine vision.

God must have felt the same
let the fallen, in the cold of gloomy pain,
love once more.
Before I lose the count of new faces I see
in the passing tram of death and war.

The Neighbour's Burnt House

Fazar azaan bellowed– *Allah O' Akbar…*

Brought the flavoured sounds of the fire wagon
wooooouuuun, woooooouuuuun
cutting through the smog.

The neighbour's house was burning
while time engulfed its fragments– of dolls
play dates and war machines.

I woke up with my hands cupping my chest
falling and rising, rising and falling
strangely exasperated.

Today the sky settled on my skin
fog like evenings– nestling
the *Myanaa*s so lost in feeding off the dead.

News broke– four-month-old raped
a Muslim lynched, Asifa-Nirbhaya
carcass meat in the blood spilled in mob assault.

Madness– running and running
away from the rumours of fear
of what no one knew, fear of whom
none understood.

Water guns hurled into the mouth of the fire
and the giant emerged stronger
lusting for more souls
hiding under the beds.

My neighbour's frozen faces made the crows
perch on four walls at a safer distance.
Silver, crimson, turquoise and peacock blue.

Dragon's fire feasted
the world was in Hell.

Dear Brother

i
Dear brother,
tonight I gather words and burn it.
How easy is it to say things?
Beside my memory a hand moves prayer beads.
It wishes to become real.

Under my feet the ground shakes,
I, in the heat of things, travel out
recollecting better things in this world.
My bucket of dreams has a hole in it;
I take the grounded earth,
mix it with my soul and mend the hole.

Can you feel the warmth in soil digging hands,
dear brother?
Aren't we all digging our own graves for a day
soon to come?

ii
Flesh and blood
bind bones to body and soul.

Is it true that sacrificing 'the self'
leads to true realization?

I never left anything for you,
dear brother,
just some lighter jokes of life.
I never shared my blood with you,
yet I leave warmth for you.

Dig it out when I shall be gone
on a long walk.
I have to walk out of life,
find few pebbles to tie my soul
so that they float around.

I can be your halo.
I can be your grief.
But, I want to be your moment of peace.

Live, dear brother, that is my gift.

Death In The Holy Month

Mother asks me to pray in the holy month,
pray for my sins and the sin ever after.

I turn to Thomas's *Conversation of Prayer*:
"The sound about to be said in the two prayers
for the sleep in a safe land and the love who dies..."

That leaves the invasive crow of the dawn
cawing away
and my consciousness rattling
in the storm again.

I am disturbed to think of death
to come once
and leave the dead hanging
in a heaven and a hell.

The lingering taste of life then invokes me:
"Souls belong to nature,
mixing in earth, sky, fire and water,
and thus, no more of it."
What if her grey-haired soul marred with insomnia,

his innocent blood-clotted hands frozen after birth,
and the soul of those whom I didn't love or hate,
are the breeze and starlight?

Shall I become the same prayer
and ease those who live,
without knowing the true nature of death and life
and be as I am- the everlasting words.

Thomas turns in his grave and reads his *Sullen Art*:
"*...From the raging moon I write*
on these spindrift pages...
but for the lovers...who pay no praise or wages..."

And I look at the sullen moon brighter than ever,
tonight I am praying to my soul for the answers.

Home Is Not An Empty Island

Foraging inside the dew drops that fell from darkness,
I found solace,
the word 'solace' imprinted in every cell of its being,
never dissolving, never melting away.

It was strange to see it hold its ground, its existence so firmly.

It was like sunlight on wet moss,
calm and living in the warmth of its home.

In it dreams floated and my soul
floated in the foliage of those dreams.
The bubble of hope wrapped around it like a child
to a mother and lifted it to the sky.

Water to air, air to water,
soil to soul, soul to soil,
everything travels.

The breeze was as cold as ice,
fiercely blowing to the south,

to the mountains where clouds make love and it rains.

I become the maple leaf then and
hold the homeless droplets together,
home is not an empty island anymore.

Eulogy Of Dreams

Time, I reluctantly see you play
with the heartbeats of dreams.
They are not yours to claim and fiddle with.

Each thought is a drop of sesame
in the silver of the moon,
running in the hourglass
dawn to dusk and dust to storm,
desiring a handful of soil to pass through and exist.

Above body and flesh
the eyes travel to a town called Hope.
It is the most harmless thing to make a home in.

Solitude of hours find the translucent worries,
merely ripples in the pond where frogs procreate
and leave nothing but a race of mechanical lovers.
The soul though feels the vibrations

of impulsive thoughts
that moves the pigeons
to fly and the kites to sail higher.

Eulogy of dreams
marks the agitated mind with a peaceful silence.
Until sunlight settles on the bosoms of wisdom,
breaking the glass and dissolving
everything beyond understanding.

Surmedani

Leukonychia of my nails are the first sighs
of the *Muharram* moon.
I wipe the slate clean
write 100 names of gratitude–
and a storm. Humanity was drowning and
I was saving my soul.

Mournful cry throbbing on the walls,
hamseera, my soul sister,
pictures of the living or dead–
closes the doors of *rehmat.*
I drew a world without humans.

Ripples in the sky's vacuum.

Why did my eyes want to shut off?
Why my charcoaled heart sealed away
the mahogany wooden bed
under which I had played home-home?

I carefully opened a *Surmedani–*
copper moulded *surahi*

that a sacred pilgrim,
had procured from a pilgrimage to *Mecca*,
in 1996.

I was half to her knee,
half in her wisdom;
she knew it could bring out–
the hidden sorrows.

The pigeons on the porch of my pupils,
meditated on one leg,
all day long.
Three times in each–
the powdered kohl-rich in coolness,
burned the hollows of my eyes.

Floods eating away a thousand graves
empty homes had no one to call its own
and for the first time,
I remembered the taste of kohl tears.

Believe That My Skin Smells Of Uprooted Longings

Believe that my skin smells of uprooted longings
and my touch leaves behind–
a nostalgic aftertaste in undiscovered corners
of the body.

Believe that my voice makes words
float in a day of odd thoughts
until 'the self' settles on insomniac breathings–
the moon shrinks into a sun
and the stars dissolve in my palms.

Believe that inertia of my loss
is new blood to the numbing mechanical mind;
falling off is just another excuse
for stubborn ideals to run faster
and my flashed striking pain
a cause to inspire all.

Believe that the colour of my feet is turquoise blue
bathing in salty tears
of the never ending war of egos;

the sparkle in my eyes
is the numbness of feelings
and my spirit is a blue rose forever loved by a unicorn
grazing in your neighbourhood.

Believe that my tongue has tasted silence
feeding on the flowers in the wail of beauty
cradled in God's hands;
my impulsive heart of reasoning
has found a traveling home
and my insecurity is a fictional character
always holding your fears in a box of love.

Believe all that I say and all that I show,
until you believe in the existence of faith in yourself
and the faith in the workings of the universe.

Deafening Noise

There is too much noise sometimes
deafening noise,
if Pain was an asylum,
I was its only inmate
surrounded by the maddening noise.

Is noise white or black
or specks of grey in a hair?

Is it like wisdom or disdain
or is it a place of realization or seclusion?

I don't understand
I don't want to know
knowing it all increases conflicts and contradictions
and then the thoughts speak
without ever stopping to think of the noise.

Massive noise–
strongly displacing the realities of dreams
and the acceptance of peaceful listening.

I want to listen now
so talk if you know how to talk.

Talk not for discovery or follies of others,
talk for the abundance of love.
Intangible like air yet warm like dreams
so it pains less in the pricking noise.

Letters To 'The Self'

i
Dear Self,
you know, life is a question to me.
And desires caging my heart, a board game.
Today I stand in thick mud
holding nothing but sorrow
tomorrow I will hold pain.

But some dreams lead me to no-man's land,
where I am a stranger to strange people.
You see, I have been a puppet
with no place to call home-
and no soul to love
yet I have sunken deep in emptiness of hope.

Will it ever leave me to feel the blossoms of summer
and live in the rains of winter?
I know not why mind can't understand
the depth of prayers?

I keep praying for the violent voice
willing to trample the ego of 'the self'

yet they raise arms against the innocent.
You know, I have travelled from the moon
to the sun and beyond,
looking for a sea shell.
I heard that they died in war of conflicts.

ii
Dear Self,

Stories are for the world that has lost all hope
I have lost faith in humanity.

There is a wide trench of hollowness
in the feelings of love and hate.
But they have taken everything away from me
even the desire to dream.
yet the shade of my soul is white in speckles of grey.

Eating me from bone to soul
until I couldn't see the reality anymore.
I wish we remain strangers as long as
time can bear the worries of the future.

I go for really long walks
with the hope of leaving–
my peaceful kites for birds and beast
because humans aren't humans anymore.

They are termites hiding behind
made up images,
waiting to wage war.
I travel in and out of myself
glad you are travelling in the universe,

today I have to prepare for a funeral.

No, not of the body but of the mind
I am writing on the mellowed leaves,
feel the burning sensation
I can meet you in dreams though.

Perceive

Perceive that the shade of my skin –
olive, crimson, purple, and lemony green.
Yet the shade of my soul is white in speckles of grey.

Too hot, too cold
my ligaments and senses either way burn
and I live with it.

The skeleton is raw earth.
The organs are pure water.
The senses are wild nature,
but to people–
I am only made of blood and bones.

I wonder and wander–pole to pole
searching and preaching.
If God taught humility, you taught to deceive
and divide in the name of politics and religion alike.

You never can know,
people are people–

humane and outrageous at the same time.

My mind though perceives something beyond
colours and creeds of deeds
it looks for a space to be as it is.

No pretence, no credence
just an ignited light
holding the burned ashes to solemn stars.

Let me too have a path of reasoning and reclaim the lost lives,
reclaim the colour of sensible and sensitive perspectives.

White Flower

Only a few breaths left
death clouded the burdened souls
his comrades fell dead.

War
a cunning plan
glorified.

On the mountain of bodies
white flowers in hand,
she stood again, a silent spectator.
Her hollowed eyes, dry and lifeless,
saw through his horrible dreams.

As cannons, guns and mad men
blew the world to pieces.

His vision fading away
to a chosen doomsday,
when guns had tip-toed through the graves
of thousand scarred tombs.

Once prime and full of dreams
covered with blood-soaked white flowers
thundering the echoes and sobs
of mothers cursing men of war.
The guns shot again and the little flowers fell
and she kissed the dead soldier
one last time.

Sealed in her bottle of shame—
a handful of blood dust,
a white flower,
souls of the dead,
a piece on peace remained
penned down as a prayer.

By the child, perhaps a poet,
her mocking laughter echoed.

War a game of fools
death a flaw of fate
claiming only the innocent.
The world slept in peace
as we, humanity, died at war.

God is Falling

God is falling in your hands,
your blow fatal to His beliefs.

Clinging onto decay,
you tear His world apart.
Bit by bit lighting love into
the fire of hell that consumes you.

God is tired now–
His lesson of harmony
long forgotten, bury His
tolerance with the dead you killed.

Did He divide you?
Did He ever tell you to
rage war and chaos?
Energies of love and hate,
equally dwell in His universe.
God is falling into your dark intentions.

His heart tears into pieces
seeing your fall.

When will you be tired
of this war against your
own kind?
War against harmony.

When will you live in peace?

Insomniac Breathings

Living in the city of wakefulness
I assume it's the trick of the sleepless stars—
captivate the feverish dreams.

Who has known?
Who will ever know?

The secrets of the eternal knowledge of
the insomniac breathings
that binds the haunting eyes
night after night and fixes itself
on the parchments of the eyelids.

Time is stubborn enough
cruel enough to settle cross-legged
on the lap of emptiness that finds solace in the body.

I circle the delirious reality of dreams
and the screams of painful silence.
I realize the secret is locked in an ice age of the mind.

Shifting the oceanic tears

from the green continent of hope,
the murky island of useless purposes floats away.
Until all is forgotten on the placid roads of life
and insomnia lives on.

Forgetful Fragments

I.
I met with an accident
a few broken limbs here and there
skull leaks suicidal fantasies
and I keep floating.
For a moment nothing mattered
for a moment I didn't exist.

Outside the window—
life stopped.
Was it waiting for me to walk the sidewalks?
It felt good to forget my name.
Is it not the nature of things
to erase the memory of existence?
I am to be erased soon.

II.
I keep forgetting
why an image of my

younger self looks happy?
I look away when my eyes
meet my smile in the mirror
that cannot hide reality.

III.
If I had no face,
if I had no skeleton,
if I had no frame of mind,
if I had no soulful heart,
if I had nothing of the above,
I would have had still *me*
left to ponder upon the *me*
that has been forgotten.

IV.
I am asleep yet
my eyes stare at the
broken light across the street.
I wake up from my grave
to breathe a little
when no one is looking.

Could I have written
my own eulogy?
I wonder why I forget
what I could have become.
When the world claimed
I had a hard soul,
I agreed and left for a higher plane.

Love Marks

I.
Bubbles at the end of
my sour drink,
brewing storm of self-respect.
Some words have watermarks,
some have spines.

I wander in the bubbles
leaving your lip.
Cheers to the days that
we live without each other,
for now enjoy our walks
together, love.

II.
I wrap your lip mark
in a tissue paper,
I hold it longer to
let it mark my destiny.
Somewhere, you leave
your kiss on a child,
innocent and pure.

In a dream, I kiss a blue
bird lost in the clouds
in another dream, you plant
a beating heart.

III.
Last sip of love slipped from my lip
and fell in my tears
swimming to the other side.
I gather the broken chalice spilling my belief.

First, it rained in January
songs of separation.
Today the land is dry.
Hold it when it's fresh
just out of naked feelings,
simmer it slow on passion
until love is a ripe mango.

Yellow Of Summer

Tread lightly, lest you
crush the yellow of summer
under your hasty steps.
If you were the leaf and I was
your leap of faith,
a curious hand would
have caught our curious fall.

Fingers reconcile with
old tales of blood bonds again,
one hurt, the other mourns in vain.

A child laughs at our childish fights,
an old hand you seem
to have held when a boy had died.

An old clock, starts ticking
somewhere in a cultured home
where lives of strangers meet.

I still look for your laughter
when eyes fall out of life,

perhaps someday we can
find the lost spring flowers under the trees,
running to catch them alive.

And you were right to say once,
"We should live in the yellow of summer."

Diagonal

The protruded belly of the yellow walls
in the bylanes,
smelled of nostalgic festive fragrance.

A sip of the orange bubbly—
khasphool and peach,
taste of memory in my mouth.

Red earth-dusted hands opening the rusty lock
of *Qamrunkhala's* door,
the checkered evening brought
the blue flower dressed girl
in the front seat of my table.

The table of a diagonal *Mandala*.

Circle

Ice-water gathered in the Moroccan tea coaster
overlooking the word *peace* on the circular wall,
I was accused of pain.

I poured it in a glass bottle where God resides.

Angular

I draw an angular shape,
leaving space for light
and shade darkness.

The lizard hiding under the papaya
branch eyes its prey,
far lights follow angular lines
around the peach sky.

In the middle—
azaan and *arati* find the same voice.

Separation

I separate things
into bits and pieces,
things this heart
cannot fathom, and
this mind cannot churn.

I peel the lip
promising separation
and plant a thorn instead,
I see you bleed.

Are you for real?

You believe in love–
possessed hearts,
I smoke rolled love letter cigarettes
letting it simmer slowly
and puff.

Limb to torso, spine to ribs,
you make a thin cut and search
the heart,

that tore the notions of true love,
mine beats in the box on display.

Craft a paper heart instead
out of dreams,
tell me when had you loved last.
It's tricky
to love a hundred
hearts than one,
to write hundred
notes of separation than one.

Flirtation

You pass your coffee,
I sip your last elixir.
Your eyes not your own
but that of a passing
speck of grey
binding my black
to the white of sex.

No I do not love or
lust for you,
no I do not crave to
be complete.
I long for the last drop
of black, rusty, ruthless,
romantic, aromatic,
coffee.

I see the last glimpse
of the brown sun
shredding the last bit
of the monotonous
life in me.

I dab the hard liquor and
paint with your resuming,
exhuming, presuming
eyes that looks
at the dropping last drop
of coffee from my lips
to the cup,
from the cup to the table,
from the table to the floor
where it mixes with the earth.

The brown with the black,
the black with the grey and
the grey with the white
of flirtatious coffee.

My Paper Dolls

You see,
I have played with paper dolls,
the scary not so perfect yet adorable dolls.

Each cut perfectly hanging from the
disjointed limbs of the subconscious self.

To a child
a paper doll means everything.
It doesn't have a gender, a caste, a colour
but later the sexist pour inside her being something
and the child changes with the doll.

Speaking to me tides of timeless sufferings,
dolls of paper heart plastered everywhere I see now.

You see,
they have no reasoning nor self satisfaction,
certainly lesser sensibilities
created their hollowness.
But my paper dolls speak the truth,

they too had shaped the world once.

We sit on the clouds often listening
to the whispers of paper souls.
Passing each lacuna and measuring
their depths.
What if the stars too were made of paper?
Will it too receive the perceptions of the forgotten
paper dolls?

A Poet's Home

You stand in the middle of fading four walls,
backside to the half-broken door,
looking for something.
Walls that smell of old books,
all dusty, all suffocated,
are your enemies.

Brewing coffee of countryside,
your eyes speak out
about the open sky.

Your silent weeping nights,
weaving words
by the bedside
of a poet's home—
loses its meaning.

You look beaten,
your footprint fading
with time.

Memory of an old love,

in every corner of your
bookshelf,
gathers love notes.

Only to let you return
to your words,
to your dreams,
to your soul,
to a poet's home.

How I Killed Love

Love birds, so in love
peck and please,
each other in my iron cage.
I separate the two,
I see one screams and
one submits to my doing.

Days, weeks, months pass,
screaming gives way
to longing;
submission gives way to
cries,
love gives way to sorrow.

I still wait for something
to stir my heart,
to separate the dead emotions with hate or love.

I feel nothing to see
them suffer,
they still feel my
suffering.

I control love
that travels around
the cage,
where each night the love birds
write letters of separation.

I write after a decade
how I killed love that
never left the cage,
that never left my
stoned heart,
that never left the beating
affections of the love birds.

I Felt The Earth Beneath Your Feet

I felt the earth beneath
your feet shaking,
some foretold your fall.
In a dark broken-down
staircase,
a haunted soul saw you climb
the ladder of hope.

Climb it dear poet,
walk to the glass window,
see words have returned
to the chair of dreams.

Count your heartbeat
as it rises,
your hand cupping your
restless soul,
shall see the sun melt
in your palms soon enough.

Let the rat race end,
let the earth shake minds to be mindful of words.

Somewhere breeze
brushed a passing verse,
slowly whispering thoughtful words to silent ears.

Nothing can change the
course of destiny,
it was written long before you were born.

Watermark Of Life

i.
I gazed in the watermark of life,
no I wasn't looking for my other self.
A moment ago I was dangling
between conscious and conscience,
constantly cornering perception in
the white washed window walls.
Behind it something stirred
my yellow flowers and it rained.
In the pool that gathered around the pigeons,
I saw my footprints walking towards today,
walking through the moment.

ii.
It's been a while since the sky died,
now all I see is unwavering greenish dullness.
A silence that never can change
and somewhere deep inside,
my emptiness is craving a rainy sky.

Perhaps the sullen calls give it hope.

A dull day can be outstretched with colours
and painted skillfully across the parallel
windows that don't open at all.
I see a pigeon building a nest.
Is this perfectly all right?

iii.
The night pours over the sullen feathers of a pigeon,
I feel the pangs of rain.
Hesitantly, I reach out,
I let go, I step forward.

The barricades of rigidity–
the iron rod proclaims the night.
Fluttering feathers wet with desire
look for a shoulder once more.

Diseases Unknown

On my right, an angel counts my days of life,
on my left, crickets sing symphony of death.

My body is an abode of diseases unknown–
a mouse tail runs in my breasts,
a nerve swells up my brain,
a ligament thickens the spine
and my legs freeze in wild dreams.

Am I withering away into oblivion?

Like thoughts suddenly disappearing
in transition of memories.

Grief has weight too,
I didn't know it did.

So is pain bonded in medallions of superstitions?
Hoping to heal the heart and the soul.

I walk with a stick in my garden,
a window to my paradise,

something earthy enough to feed
my weakening strength some soothing verses.
I root myself to a tree waiting to grow taller
enough to shed the heaviness of pain and
be home with the mysterious healing stream.

Frostbitten Revolution

My frostbitten fingers
dipped pen in bloody snow
to write songs for you, Lara.
Snowflakes on white glass
melted far away
in the land of hope.

Hunger,
a new disease,
unhappy men off to war.
Wolves howled and feasted on cold flesh,
leftovers of death.

I witnessed it all.

Red guard, white guard.
Who guards humanity?
Revolution you brought doom,
you brought hate and suspicion,
snow-caked lanes were witness of your unholy affairs.

Lara, tell me,

"How did you come to be so lost?"
A whip on the horse carriage
and we travelled through life.

Sunflower petals withered slowly,
a spring child in her bosom,
a poet on her trail,
lost again and again.

Lara brought poetry to me,
so hopeful, so beautiful.

Two extreme emotions,
love and hate, hope and despair;
but the world needs light Lara,
the light of an innocent vision.

The vision of poetry,
the verse of poets,
nobody loves poetry more than the mad,
perhaps we shall meet beyond this madness.

Dear Lara, let me survive
to meet you in another life.
Until then I'll ban verses.

Revival

Dead end.
Is this how one fine day everything ends?
Past or present nothing makes sense,
I wrote your name Poetry,
in a thousand ways I did try to understand you.

But how do I know myself?
How do I accept dead end?
Poetry do you ever feel anything at all?
I expressed myself through you,
I laid you bare, out in the open for show.

Did I shame you then?
I am afraid I can't make you eternal,
there is no such thing as eternity.
I die, you die with me.

Once in a while on a dead day,
you and I will be discussed boringly,
an audience with half interest, half asleep,
would curse our revival.

Su.11

Would you ever live like that?
Isn't dead end a relief?
Both to dust shall travel,
in the roots of trees shall breathe,
to see one world crumble and another rise,
in the dead end of life.

My Body Is A Pile Of Papers

My body is a pile of papers left behind on a bench,
fold and unfold-shape and reshape,
the mystery in the hands of imagination–a child.
I wouldn't want anyone else to find my body
and the restless soul caged inside it,
its desires are beyond permitted wishes.
How can we control everything and anything beyond us all?
A child is beyond hesitating and fearful norms–
beyond control.

Into a paper plane he shapes me,
the folds so fine I can see how the world looks from above,
so majestic yet so irrelevant.

Into a ship I then become
and another sheet becomes a dragon.
I have legs and wings to carry the ship as far as I want to,
sailing on the strength and wonder of a child,
braving the waves and finding the horizon.

He gives it to the passers-by, not noticing
anything at all in their commercial strides.

A paper rose I delicately become not for a lover
but for a grave,
perhaps a soul parted ways and
I keep the bond alive to last the summers.

A storm warns his senses and
twists my soul into a kite,
and spring birds urging to return home
stir my tail to feel the wind alive.
An envelope later he shapes me into and
writes a long letter to the Nobodys,
one for the paperwala, one for chaiwala,
one for the school teacher, one for the policeman
and one for his mother in heaven.

He plays and sings and I become the stories within him.

Neatly shades of my soul gets distributed,
words and words of love to fill the emptiness
of lives lost in the chaos.
One he keeps to himself and writes:
Why people live to die in the end?
Why kill humanity if you want to die inhuman?
Why not live in peace and die for love?
And he sends me to God to find the answers
we all used to believe in.

Tolerant Kisses

In muffled kisses babies are born,
bastards are born in the storms of summer.
I wondered whether rain and spring children had a chance
ever to cleanse doubts and differences so consuming the
minds.

Winter only birthed cold heads full of superstitious
nerves that burned reasoning
and autumn child like me always wandered on the road
collecting the reminiscences of a healing leaf.

I see all drank the same holy water but
not all thought good of each other and I felt the nerve
pull.
I carry the pain in my legs and
my body in the hope of catching when their heads fall,
and kiss them all goodbye.

Not to bury them in the black hole
but under the humane earth to let them
grow again at the same time,
the time of tolerant kisses of love.

Existential Search

Only the Moon's touch feels the emptiness
of the large room I live in.

The lady in the dark ties and unties the knots
from the string of moon beams,
the head and tail of the coin on her palm
tested her impatient imperfections.

I didn't have the will to question,
"Why was she feeling lost in the vast range of thoughts?"
Was she puzzled about the feeling
of living alone in darkness of existence?

Casually moulding the clay in her palms
to make a new shape of a stone
to hold loneliness of longings.
I know it can soak the darkest black of souls
leaving only numbness of being lost behind.

She cried when nothing made sense,
a catharsis to my wandering eyes
or another overgrown existentialist search,
I pondered.

So What Is A Poem?

So what is a poem?
A somber soliloquy of sentiments
or an escape of naked nights;
or the parting of memories,
or a memoir of a journey.

So what is a poem?
A splash of ethereal consciousness
or a thrust of forceful repartee;
or a feeling of knowing it all,
or a sound of a lost voice.

So what is a poem?
A question with infinite possibilities
or a beating of words together to form a shape;
or an extension of a hand towards self discovery,
or a walk in the genre of compartmental fancies.

Do you now know what a poem is?
Can you differentiate word from phrases and pick up
the message?

Would you now reread thoughts again and change
what is necessary?
So that you can explain to me about the essence of
poem within a poem.

Insanity

A mad man paints Christ on the unpaved roads,
on a high he overlooks
the ogling disgusted eyes.
Marijuana mixed in his pee–
a high doze to forget.
In his palms the world appears,
one deep drag and the illusionist disappears.

He forced his insanity on me,
to take it and throw away.
His filthy hands, his broken jaw,
his rags raged unknown storms.
Sweaty and smelly,
a rotting mass of insanity
spoke out loud,
"I am lost, so is my insanity,
take it, take it,
I never want to see it."

Cursing my very being,
at my puzzled looks he laughed,
I didn't accept like him my sane insanity.

No God, no Lord,
rain overflowed through him,
sitting on his hindsight,
only a penny for the enraged tummy.

A penny dropped,
circled around and fell flat,
thoughts ran wild like his hunger.
Can he eat this penny?
But it's of no value,
nothing can be bought,
not even a morsel of bread.

Gathering his own filth and
his decayed body,
he walked to a higher ground.

What a fool to say so?
I am civilized unlike him,
but he is free unlike me.
And nothing can take away
the peace in chaotic insanity,
not even a lost sane like me.

Towards My Home

Give me a home that isn't mine.
In between space and infinity,
longing for the journey stands on the edge
calling and my search continues.

A shadow under night's fall
is more known to me than the strangeness of the
soul,
walking bare in wild chaos of the mind
to hold onto the body's cage.

Each breath,
a disguise in hope to sail the sand
and hide in a cocoon to free the heart
to find a home.

Not in imagination but in the tides
of moonlight and the symphony of water.

I pack my baggage in my feet,
climbing towards tomorrow,
towards my home.

The Colour Of Mourning Isn't Black

The colour of mourning isn't black,
soot in the air soiling my tears
celebrates another death,
I realize nothing is forever.

Hazing away the last glimpse of the sun,
the void appears clearer.
Familiar with the passing of breath
yet unfamiliar with the feel of life.

Unable to let go of the fragile bond
binding the flesh to the soul,
the fist grows restless.

Have you ever observed that in a dark room
the speck of light looks starved?
Its strange notion of living inside
the ever-growing cotton seed,
baffles my reasoning.

I could never hold a hummingbird in my palm,
too afraid it will die a natural death.

So much pain in hate I see,
so much loss of clarity
confining the soulful pursuits.

I often live outside my head to see
what remains oblivious to death.

Death of prayers,
slowly eating away the flower of peace.

www.ingramcontent.com/pod-product-compliance
Lightning Source LLC
Chambersburg PA
CBHW052014170626
46808CB00007B/2926